THE END OF A BEGINNING:
Musings on Forestalled Love

By:

RACHEL W. ROBINSON

FALL 2021

Contents

Unknowing

I don't know why you did what
you did
Why you didn't do what you
didn't do
Why you thought what you
thought
Didn't think what you want

Didn't believe what you knew

Letting others infiltrate your
mind
Ignoring my answer when you
asked "Are you mine?"

It all could have been so simple
But we made waves out of
ripples

Confusion caused by insecurity
Chaos in our infinity

Full of potential never fully born
A spark of a flame
Not enough to keep us warm
Because you were always torn

Refused to believe
That I could be really yours

You always doubted
So why not let me go?
I never pushed, pulled, or
shouted
Your intuition kept you close

But the false stories in your
mind
Kept you closed

Secrets are the destruction of
truth
Darkness, the destruction of light
But the heart is the sun
Illuminating the darkness of the
mind

Feel it. Follow it.

Dear Twin Flame

Dear Twin Flame,

You're at war with the darkness
Searching for my light
The key is there inside you
Unlock your heart to release
your mind

Silence is not the enemy
But a gift in disguise

Quiet the noise
Listen to God's voice
He will guide you to my side

We'll fight this war together
Hand in hand
Stride by stride
We've been fighting for this
forever
It becomes clear
When you open your eyes

Step out of the darkness
Into your power
Fully embody the Sacred Flame
No more secrets, no more hiding
No more lies, no more shame

Burning with passion for me
And for life and for Truth
Burning away the pain

By allowing it to flow through
you

The love we share is healing
For us and for the World
An Eternal Twin Flame
Scorching away the evil of the
Earth

There are no limitations
No boundaries that can keep us
apart
The obstacles are an illusion
We are connected by the Heart

Our Soul has always been united
In vibration and intent
Our bodies may be separate
But our Soul cannot forget

The many lifetimes we have
spent as One
Exploring and learning to evolve
There is no boundary that we
cannot overcome
No opposition that we cannot
dissolve

If it is our fate to be together in
this life
Then that is what we will do

But even if it is not
Please know

That I will always love you.

And I know that you will always
love me, too.

Aquarian Love Song

The reason I can love so easily
Why my feelings flow and
abound
Is just as quickly as I jump in
I can jump out

It's a switch that turns on and off
And when I am on
No one compares

But turn me off
See how fast I run
Leaving you wondering why life
is so unfair

Fully alive
Feeling everything around
Because no matter how many
times I fall
I never hit the ground

Life is to be lived
Love is to be given
When I have so much inside me
I'm the one you will be missin'

I can make anyone feel special
Doesn't mean that they are
It is my curious nature
But I never lower the bar

I giveth and I take away
It is the Goddess within
Fully embodied in my power
My original sin

Is to know my true value
And therefore live with no fear
I come, I see, I conquer
Yet you still long to be near

To bask in the sun
That is my divine light

To create everything around me
That is my divine right

While you dream about me
every night

You grasp at the memories
That swirl around in your mind
My touch, my body
You see me every time you close
your eyes

Your prototype

But no one who comes after me
will be ever the same

You will look for me everywhere

I won't even remember your
name.

4

Darling

The reason I'm so youthful
Why I'm so happy and free
Is that I choose well
And I allow myself to see

You either want me or you don't
You either convince me to stay
Or I leave
You either satisfy my curiosity
It's a very simple life that I lead

There is no tug-of-war
You pull too hard
I cut the string

They say love is a battlefield
But for me
Love is like Spring

A new beginning
I'll only fall
When I find my King

In his arms
I will blossom
Like the nightingale
I'll sing

But it takes a special man
To truly bring that out in me

Sure I've loved and
Made others fall in love with me
Knowing they weren't quite
right
I was only practicing

Harmless sparring partners
In the battle for my heart
I can let them believe they have
won
Because the battle never really
starts

But a King captures me with a
look
Sets me free with a touch
I find myself at his mercy
I can never have too much

And he can never have enough.

That is the story of love
That I've written time and again
That I've lived and breathed and
enjoyed
That has kept me fulfilled to the
end

Love need not last forever
But for me it must be real
And I have had the best loves
To last several lifetimes
They are the reason I am
unafraid to feel

The reason I live with childlike
abandon
The reason I live life with such
joy
The reason why you really can't
hurt me

Darling,

You are merely a boy.

30 Days

A blink of an eye
In the scheme of my life
While the spark of our flame
Will forever flash in your mind.

You thought I would chase you
That I would beg for your time.
But I just created an opportunity
For you to change my mind.

30 Days is nothing.
I will easily forget.
But the time you didn't spend
with me,
Is time that you will regret.

30 Days was just a test.

A sample.

For me to see
How life with you would taste.
I really didn't like it
So there was no more time to
waste.

30 Days of nonsense
And all your foolish games.
I can't believe you thought you
had me.

Did you really think that was the
way?

30 Days of flirtation
And fun and laughs and sex.
Yeah, we said we were exclusive

But I don't even consider you to
be an ex.

30 Days of nothing.
Empty words and empty dreams.
Empty games that were based on
Empty thoughts and empty
beliefs.

Did you think they were real to
me?

That must be it.

30 Days of confusion
But you weren't confusing me.
I played along
I learned the script
And then decided to retreat.

To go back to being with Me.

Much better company
If I'm honest, which I always
was
So 30 Days for me brought
clarity
and more self-love.

But what did it bring for you?

Another notch on your belt?
But for whom to see?
Bragging rights?

But who brags about losing me?

It's silly. Laughable really.

The Wrong Choice

Don't you know that I can hurt
you
In just enough ways
To make you want me more

But you would never hate me
You would crave me
Just as much as you crave the
war

Because any attention
Is good attention
Until my attention is no more

I could make you beg
For the suffering
Because you can't bear
To see me walk out that door

But you don't have to suffer,
Darling
And that is what you truly know
A life with me would be full of
happiness
Even when we go through
storms

So then why do you choose this
chaos?
Why do you test my resolve?
You must know that I will leave
And in the silence
Your sins will never be absolved.

It makes no sense,
My Sweetheart
When you know I cannot be
fooled.

I know when you are at your
best.
You seem to think I can be
subdued.

But I can't.

I always see the truth.

A Lesson From The Wise

The more open you seem
The more naïve people believe
you are
Is the quicker they show you
Who they really are

Because they don't think they
have to hide it
They think they can string you
along
They forget their mask
They reveal themselves
Because they don't think that
you'll catch on

So this is what you did to me
Fooling yourself all along
Believing the sweet nothings I
whispered to you
And now you're angry that I'm
gone?

That I could see so clearly
What was going on?
That I could handle the truth
And move on?

So this is a lesson from the wise
The true test of those around you:

The way you treat those you
believe you can take for granted
Shows the evil that surrounds
you.

While the sweetness confounds
you.

True power is making others
love you;
To be blameless in their eyes.
Then every time they close
them,
Their guilt takes over their mind.

Forever bound to their suffering
And wondering why

How could she escape?
How could she not believe my
lies?

Is that what you wonder
When you close your eyes?

Darling, I'm older and wiser.
This is your lesson from the wise.

The End of A Beginning

Is that what you were afraid of?

That I would make you love me
and then I would leave?
That you would be left with
nothing to show besides our
memories?

That you would be left with only
questions?
With pain without reprieve?
That you would be left alone in
the dark
Licking your wounds in grief?

That I would move on and never
think twice
Of the time I spent with you?
That I would forget and find joy
with another?

That what we had was never
true?

If that is the case,
Then answer me this:
Isn't that what you made me do?

You ended our beginning.

I thought I saw my life with you.

Rejection

Rejection is not protection
When you get rejected by me
Rejection is a symptom
Of your toxic energy

I love all people
And enjoy when people love me
So if I don't want you around
Clean off your mirror
So you can see

Sittin' pretty in my Empress
energy
You won't get past my guards
Unless I approve what you're
offering

If you can't see past the fog
Of your ego and shadow self
My intuition pierces your smog
Divinity guides me to leave you
on the shelf

Love for me is simple
It flows and ebbs and heals
Make me wonder too many
questions
And I will disappear

Life for me is easy
I ask and I receive
Try to take away my joy
I will very quickly leave

It's a very big gamble
To let me walk away
Because for me
The past is the past
And if I'd wanted you
I would have stayed

Would have convinced you
To see things my way
Would have seduced you
With my charm
My ability to persuade

But if I found that you're not
worth it
What is left for us to say?
You want me to waste time
listening
To excuses for your toxic ways?

Give me a break.

I got things to do
So I'll be on my way.

A Warning

It's not me you don't trust
It's yourself
Looking for signs that you are
unworthy
While others made you doubt
What you felt

Misjudging me on superficial
nonsense
Not seeing my character within
Projecting your insecurities
Blocking a chance for this to
begin

You must realize that we've all
been hurt before
Been disappointed, heartbroken,
and torn

Been deceived, devalued, and
discarded by Love because
Like a rose, every Love has
its thorns

No one deserves to dictate your
future
No one who has hurt you before
Deserves the power to block
your happiness
You must pick yourself up off
the floor

If you do not, then you will never
know when True Love
crosses your path
And when it tries to live inside
you again
You will kill it with the past

Look up, not back, My Darling
Lift up your eyes from the
ground
Get up and keep moving
See the possibilities all around

It's the reason we are on this
planet
The reason why we can feel
The reason why you must trust
your intuition
When it guides you towards
what's real

I may not be your answer
But I hope I have given you a
glimpse
At what happiness could be like
When you free yourself
from "what ifs"

From the doubts and fears that
arise in you
From the indifference that you
hide behind
From the stranglehold that you
have on your heart
From the over reliance on your
mind

Your mind does not have the
answers
Only questions it can pose
Your heart, intuition, and
feelings
Tell you what you need to know

And yes, there is a risk of
disappointment because you don't
know where the road goes
But if you bury your seeds in the
past

Then you will never grow.

Made in the USA
Middletown, DE
11 April 2023

28509364R00018